Rodrigo Toscano's *WHITMAN. CANNONBALL. PUEBLA.* demands close reading: each precise phrase, layered reference, and intricate metaphor mobilizes a transhistorical, yet deeply situated, foray into the metapolitics of form (and formal strategies: jokes, jousts, and gestures). Spanning themes from "Imperium" to "Humanitas" in his unique demotic style, Toscano's work blends collective action and poetic diplomacy in its critique of national and hemispheric imaginaries, Hispanic representation (past and present), and an emerging new global reset. Wide-ranging, yet pliant and compact, *WHITMAN. CANNONBALL. PUEBLA.* deftly scales up and scales down the hemispheric rumor mills in the poetry metaverse, offering "combustions, pipelines, [and] canalizations of fire" that traffic and power the (often disregarded, imperceptible) aesthetic networks which define our contemporary moment.
—Jose-Luis Moctezuma, author of *Black Box Syndrome*

A geo-politic, an untamed poetics of transnational realignment, or an overloaded composter of "ethno-politico GPS" signals towards a new mytho-poetic of the Americas. Here's a poetics built out of economic flows, of multilingual contradictions, of neo or just OG-colonial hustles. A new world symphony for our utterly disoriented century, wildly satirical and utterly serious, taking us all down, especially "us," the poets, the academics, the "culture workers," struggling to to keep up with the changing world order. Forget about it! If you thought you knew what poetry "does", you were wrong. And now, even better, you still don't know, because that's what the prophetic feels like.
—Julie Carr, author of *Underscore*

PREVIOUS BOOKS

The Cut Point (Counterpath Books, 2023)

The Charm & The Dread (Fence Books, 2022)

In Range (Conterpath Books, 2019)

Explosion Rocks Springfield (Fence Books, 2017)

Deck of Deeds (Counterpath Books, 2012)

Collapsible Poetics Theater (Fence Books, 2008)

To Leveling Swerve (Krupskaya, 2004)

Platform (Atelos, 2003)

The Disparities (Green Integer, 2002)

Partisans (O Books, 1999)

WHITMAN. CANNONBALL. PUEBLA.

Cover design by Rodrigo Toscano
Cover typeface: Avenir

Interior design by Laura Joakimson
Interior typeface: Adobe Garamond Pro

Library of Congress Cataloging-in-Publication Data

Names: Toscano, Rodrigo author
Title: Whitman, cannonball, Puebla / Rodrigo Toscano.
Description: Oakland, California : Omnidawn Publishing, 2025. | Summary:
"This four-part collection of poetic fables engages the emerging field
of globo-poetics through Hispano-Americano lenses. Amid global crises
between states, and cultural destabilization manifesting across mass
popular culture and literature, WHITMAN. CANNONBALL. PUEBLA. sets out
to invigorate conversation about how the United States might adapt to a
wider hemispheric consciousness. Toscano's poems present a cultural
landscape where the Anglo-capitalist outlook is tempered-if not
subsumed-by a Greater Americas "Salamanca Humanism," which was the basis
for the 1948 United Nations Universal Declaration of Human Rights. The
book is divided into four sections that develop the idea of a Greater
Americas as hinging on negotiation between Anglo and Hispano values,
consider a potential catastrophic Anglo-American imperialism, imagine
life in a Post-Empire crisis, and compose allegories about the
historical consciousness of a people oversaturated with media"--
Provided by publisher.

Identifiers: LCCN 2025015626 | ISBN 9781632431745 trade paperback
Subjects: LCGFT: Poetry
Classification: LCC PS3570.O739 W48 2025 | DDC 811/.54--dc23/eng/20250421
LC record available at https://lccn.loc.gov/2025015626

Published by Omnidawn Publishing, Oakland, California
www.omnidawn.com
10 9 8 7 6 5 4 3 2 1
ISBN: 978-1-63243-174-5

WHITMAN. CANNONBALL. PUEBLA.

Rodrigo Toscano

OMNIDAWN PUBLISHING
OAKLAND, CALIFORNIA
2025

Contents

MAIORIS HISPANIAE

Caravels out of Cádiz

"We've hustled up the healthiest cows"

"By god's will, we anchor at Vera Cruz"

"This landholding extends out *that* way"

"Señor what's-his-name's gonna build one"

"The neophytes appear reluctant (so far)"

"The holy sacraments—all of them"

"Without battle, if possible, as decreed"

"This captain's 'confidence'—is sus"

"Señores, begin by addressing privations"

"Line 'em up, six hogs and two horses"

"*Deal*, two masons, one cook, one healer"

"At your behest and wishes, Viscountess"

"Oat and rye flour arrives by late fall"

"Another surplus of chilies and chocolate"

"These five frontier towns as pious as any"

"Ten parishes in total without water"

"Complete aqueduct by June at the latest"

"Cut the sacraments to five (by July)"

"Señor, we don't quite do it like that here"

"Andalusian ways *are* changing—daily"

"Parish rolls track all manner of trades"

"*Four* indigenous languages, kid's gold"

"A hospital in this city is the goal"

"A university in this region is the goal"

"Atlacoya's Castilian coming on strong"

"This quarried rock is the prettiest yet"

"Make a painful example of that rebel"

"Release them all, they'll return, to a man"

"Build fountains where our youth may meet"

"The fashions *are* getting rather—extra"

"Please, no more rotten Portuguese cod"

"'Avocados in all four valleys?' Do it"

"Isabela's daughter is fluent in Otomí"

"*That* bloke from Bilbao needs some sun"

"The holy mother now *looks* like us"

"Absolutely no more forced labor"

"Toltecatl studies law in Salamanca"

"Put that so-called 'duke' in chains"

"A three-day festivity for the harvest"

"Silk blouses from Fukkien via Manila"

"This here region's a warless region"

"Two bands of bandits still to subdue"

"Niño, sharpen this sword—to its limit"

"The Shanghainese trade *only* in reales"

"Sire, they call the island, California"

"Cowhide pants are all the rage now"

"The English *never* marry Africans"

"Correct, nor do they marry natives"

"Our fall armada barely avoided siege"

"These *fortalezas* pay for themselves"

"Lure the bastards into the back bay"

"Repair the fountains by springtime"

"Florid dresses twirling to florid music"

"*People*, stand back, wait for your cues"

Iberofonía

Honduras and El Salvador
at first, then Guatemala
forge a union.

After the 2nd cup of coffee
Nicaragua wakes up
shucks off Russia.

As that 2nd cup settles in
a welcomed sensation
Costa Rica joins in.

So now, aside from
"Latinx" not working
Panama gets to choose.

Meanwhile, Brazil
sneaking out of BRICS club
cavorts with Angola.

Two sips of a 3rd cup
and the Central American Union
makes Mexico frisky.

As a 3rd sip starts to hit
Argentina and Chile
fall in with Greater Brazil.

Now with legit jitters
Colombia and Panama hook up
Latinx not spoken there.

Ecuador and Peru
sheets to the wind
hop into Greater Colombia.

One extra sip is what it takes
and Uruguay, Paraguay, and Bolivia
get with Greater Brazil.

Venezuela now shucks off China
Peru shucks off the U.S.
and go with Greater Colombia.

Puerto Rico, Cuba, and *Hispaniola*
after 4th cup, get freak on
as Greater Caribbean.

Greater Columbia, Greater Brazil,
Greater Mexico, Greater Caribbean,
meet up for coffee.

São Tomé and Príncipe, Guinea-Bissau,
Mozambique, Equatorial Guinea,
Cape Verde—are cordially invited.

Spain and Portugal
also cordially invited—
Latinx not spoken here.

Capitán Peachy

Inside a fort of stone
of his own making
a pentagrammic imposition
on a bluff of an island

pacing atop its walls
peering from turrets
with searing concentration
on the restless sea

on the lookout
for the enemy—
he orders a blackberry tea
sits among the chattery

and renders the battle of the flags
on the burning plaza
of his own fancy
brusquely yet colorfully.

After the morning smoke
has dissipated
after the monumentality
baroque tinseled imagery

he pops a tweet
on Anglo Imperium's decay
how its poetry
fleets of piracy

itching for a toehold
here and everywhere
with its atomistic
cosmovision

"is demoralizing
day after day
is authoritative
year upon year"

He then deletes that tweet
in a moment of reflection
a feeling of equanimity
ecumenicalism even

Then *bristles* at that retreat!
while struggling for a synonym
for "bristle"
for an hour—

Other than that—
everything's peachy

Hemispheric Rumors

Unconfirmed rumor   they're part of the
Hispano-Americano   vast empire
the very last huffs   huffing about

Unconfirmed rumor   they're bent on
making hay out of   wide awake
or half-awake   Anglospheric aggression

Unconfirmed rumor   they're maximalist
integrationist   not giving F's about
authority of   petty nationalisms

Unconfirmed rumor   they wear red & white
Cruz de Borgoña   black T-shirts
feeling it   reasonably sexy

Unconfirmed rumor   they're agnostic towards
Pan-Indigeneity   precisely when
promulgated by   Anglospheric balkanization

Unconfirmed rumor   they're resetting
left/right paradigms   in sync with
civilizational shifts   (yeah, and attitudes)

Unconfirmed rumor   they see fortress Canada
a last bastion of   Anglo (multi-culti)
non-integrationism of   The Continent, eh?

Unconfirmed rumor   they don't want
Mexican president AMLO   demanding apologies

from Spain for   stolen gold or whatever

Unconfirmed rumor   they see Mexico as
"totalmente una fabricación"   *with* benefits
non-separable from   Honduras and Guatemala

Unconfirmed rumor that *if*   Walled-up America deems
China! an existential threat   Walled-up America (with
"BIPOCS" in high places)   might-can think Otherwise

Unconfirmed rumor   they apply high precision
Hispano-Americano lenses to   every single poem in
every issue of   American Poetry Review

Unconfirmed rumor   they are hopeful
peeps in these parts   keep humpin'
coming to their   children's best interests

Unconfirmed rumor   harmonized regional
para-personal   public poetries
might clear paths for   The Zone, cabrones

Ethno-Politico GPS

This Ibero-Zacateco
palette loader
and his equally post-tribalized
Ibero-Totonaca lady
in scrubs

are not strutting Azteca
"decolonizing the poem"
jigging ibero-phobic
at a scholarly conference
in Boston.

These two Ibero-Huastecos
in chef hats
aren't shaking down
self-effacing Anglocrats
after hours

recycling mex-revolutionary
canonic cartoons
Pinot Grigio in hand
subordination *danzas*
en route to London, Paris, Milan.

This post-tribalized Ibero-Paipai
Tlaxcalteco-allied
Aztec Imperium smashing
Huasteca Totonaca liberating
cabrón

from San Diego, Alta California
is rocking a constructivist
Ibero-Indigeno-Africano
conviction-baked mask
over a poet mask.

¡Que viva México!

¡Que viva El Virreinato de Nueva España!

¡Que viva La Intendencia de Nueva Orleans
bajo la Capitanía General de Cuba
conducido por el Virreinato de Nueva España!

Go Saints. Go Padres.

Caras y Mascaras

Whitman.
Cannonball.
Puebla.

Frigates.
Dickinson.
Shanghai.

Pound.
Ramparts.
Manila Bay.

Blackhawk.
Mac Low.
Hangar lock.

Seawolf sub.
Shange.
Dry dock.

Puma drone.
Alurista.
Landing block.

Ordnance blast.
Bay of Pigs.
Baraka.

Radar jam.
Forché.

Nicaragua.

Canonizations.
Fuel depot.
Reconnaissance.

Workshops.
Close reading.
Launching pad.

White House.
Striking range.
Renditions.

Laureate.
Pacific fleet.
Pastorals.

Affirmineity.
Askancineity.
Imperium.

What's his face.
What's her face.
What's their face.

Antarctica

Actually, I retitled this one
Mendacity's March

. .

Ok, this next one is called
Admiral Nelson

. .

And I'll be closing up with
Uruguay (a torn off "found" piece)

. .

But first, I should probably read some
Ice Shelf Gas Reserve sonnets

. .

Second thought, maybe
Bolívar, The Traitor?
should come next

. .

Alright, maybe
'Latine' Pentagon Pantoum
is a better choice

. .

Perhaps folks might prefer
Pensacola Reconquista

. .

Looks like
Camino Real Towards Nueva Orleans
is also on deck

. .

You know what, fuck it
I'm just gonna read
Sonora Lithium Deposits
(the "can't hav'em!" variations)

Chatty Cholula

Igneous rocks
smushed together
with lime & clay.

This church sits
atop a pyramid,
steadfast.

You can piss
all over them
but maybe don't.

We mean
test them
feel the layering.

Were they wood
they wouldn't stand
repeated "tests."

Rocks *repel* and
keep us bouncy
here, too.

There they are
there they've been
(there they'll be)

"*Say* something"
politics insists

"about culture"

Ok, how about
syncretism's day
is here to say.

"Say something else!"
politics demands
"about practice"

Ok—question:
how many layers
to *your* city?

One layer
can be plenty
don't walk away

Test culture
by just sitting
and chatting.

Whittling words
peels layers
from city folks.

Smushing words
a proven way
to piss away the day.

Tlaloc in Iceland

"Sure, we'll pull out the 36 palms
and replant all 36, 4 feet to the right.

A crew of 6 and 2 tractors
6 palms a day that's 6 days.

Real palms would take 8 days
still, these neoprene beauts are no joke.

Honestly, I feel colder in their presence
50 degrees at midsummer, I mean.

Tuesday works fine, no worries
sleet, sludge, whatever, we're there.

Tuesday's also my wife Thordis' first day
as local deputy for the IMTMP

The Icelandic More Than Maidens Party
was an integral part of her growing up.

The songs they sing and love, *I* love
rites of passage, cod barrels of 'em.

Very very helpful, kind of like crews
divisions of labor, emotional, bodily.

Our elder son's ILPP club has no songs
I have my doubts about that party

The Icelandic Lost Puppies Party
I mean, I guess it has a function.

Teaching Tenoch Nahuatl has been a slog
we weigh the decision every single day.

Yeah, the ILPP blocks with the IMTMP
especially when the AIPP is on the rise

The All-Icelandic Peoples Party, yup
a rally, under these palms on Wednesday.

Xochitl, our youngest, her friends are all AIPP
she might be there, I know, it's tense

especially since I affiliated with the IWSIP
the Icelandic Work & Shut It Party.

'Shut it!' or 'Shut the F up!'
our slogans are easy to remember.

Presently, the IWSIP and the IMTMP
are in talks over a whole new party.

Actually, the 'More Than Maidens Party'
is the more hardcore on labor rights.

Our precocious middle child, Omacatl
he's very attracted to their platform.

Tuesday it is, we'll be there at sunup
no, we, we make our own food, thanks."

O Monterrey

Monterrey, Nuevo León
stirring in our dreams

You sprawled out before us
<that's the waking metaphor>

Newest causeway inbound
gleaming ivory concrete

six ample lanes
flecked with quartzite

Buoyantly lavished your riches
<the metaphor picks up speed>

so that we could *feel*
not just see—your machinery

automation's meta-vistas
desire squirreling with function

First, flat streets, *then* parades
pink wigs come *after* water flow

O Monterrey, such swash
powering up bardic bots

fiction—for the fiction-proof
new percussive accent's bite

It shook us—cyberly
your shimmy up to us

summoning emerald canals
performance in piston plants

lyrics landing on neoprene
rooftop-dancing night shifters

10th floor exhibitionist
chilly mountain sweeping air

You <the metaphor settling in>
caked on the coquetry

boulevard luminous picnics
cypresses' soft sway

Helicopters hovered the Plaza
strafed narcos, washed away

Aqueducts funneling spring rain
cumuli milked to the max

accordion techno blasting
5:00 a.m.—five-line lyric

recumbent sun splashing
spliced into the ruckus

amid rising nouns and verbs
sidewalk adjectives 10 pesos

Wide-brimmed black hat

we tip your saucy way

Ta-ra-ta-toom Ta-ra-ta-toom
pops the accent—*régio*

Ka-pow pow pow
poetipoids poised in power

How harness the *output*, Monterrey
whatchu need—from NOLA*

---

*   "New Orleans, Louisiana"

IMPERIUM

Mystery Reader

Downplaying entanglements
>with national interests
>and global affairs

Blurring the lines
>between transparency
>and obfuscation

This poet, nonetheless
>seems pumped enough
>to flip scrips

This poet, maybe
>is para-national
>or infra-national

This poet, actually
>speaks from metropoles
>to metropoles

Signaling new virtues
>counter-signaling others
>unlocking impulses

This poet is—*jimmying*
>(cracking codes to)
>people's minds

Toggling non-pleasurables
>to pleasurables

across frontiers

This poet is *dial-turning*
    mass-body hokum
    into source code

Tracking realignments
    between power blocks
    and cultures

Decoding goodwill
    and bad faith
    recoding trust

This poet, likely bops
    from scene to scene
    sourcing hype

Is this poet an agent
    or double agent
    for change?

Growly (global barfly)

Gibraltar—
nobody names their kid, "Gibraltar."

Gibraltar—is a *Hong Kong*.
who names their kid, "Hong Kong"?

Guantanamo and *Falkland*—
are now bald as cannonballs.

Guantanamo
spent a lifetime
sparking up awkward conversations.

Falkland
sits at the end of the bar
distance-flirting with—"Formosa"
Formosa! changed names
back when,
goes by *Taiwan*
("Malvinas"—after 12:00 a.m.)

(Ok, maybe *somebody*
did name their kid, "Falkland"
that would be pumpkiny
sweet chocolatey
strawberry rum-like)

Gibraltar
strolls into the joint
looking captainly

swivels its neck
spots *Hong Kong*
winks at *Hong Kong*.

11:59 p.m.

Now, *Taiwan*—

(Ok, maybe somebody
did name the kid, "Guantanamo"
in a pinch, on the fly)

Taiwan—
slinks out
from behind the velvet curtain
lowers its eyes—
flings back its head—

BARFS

on *Gibraltar*...

Now what?

"*Hong Kong* raises a tall glass"

Then what?

"*Guantanamo*—pretends not to see,
Falkland—bolts for the door."

Is that it?

"The crusty regular, named *Growly*
raises a tall glass back."

44

Golf Cart

Scuttled poem—
was called "Golf Cart"

Something about
Golf Cart Stage
Imperialism
ditched
in a pond.

Poem kicked off with
the cringe quatrain:

"All aboard!
here we go—
uh, little bit of a
puddle, here"

Poem sputtered out
at the next quatrain:

"Legs up!
everybody, *um*
—jump!
paddle, paddle"

Scuttled poem—
gurgling, still.

It's going to be ok.

There were no odes to doorlessness
nor hymns to windowless wondrousness.

There *could have been* tortured metaphors
with straining semaphores
to Niger, Burkina Faso, Mali,
Nigeria, Benin, and Chad.

There could have been paeans
to the latest French designs:
Le Grand Lisse, Le Magnifique Lent
L'Incroyablement Silencieux.

There could have been cold-eyed contrasts
to Russian knockoffs like
Velikiy Slavianskiy Sekret Amfibianoidov
"Great Slav Stealth Amphibianoid"

But scuttled poems
make for dubious intel
despite
encrypted lines like:

The verdant fields
in front
are unfolding

The withered fields
behind
are fast fading

It's—ok—
or, *not* ok—
either way

There *is* no breezy way
of jumping out.

What remains is
not a red wheelbarrow
in the rain

but a Golf Cart
in the muck

with its last say—

as we walk away.

Clearing Lines

"Boys in a tank
incinerated
behind a treeline"

That's as far as it got
that poem—

And alongside that fragment
—in chicken scratch:

Variate 10 times
14 syllables—per strophe
in tercets

Questionable directive—
in light of

"Boys in a tank
incinerated
behind a treeline"

This shard—

This fleck of ineffability

If unhoused by a poem
mortifies

If fully housed by a poem
doubly so...

Guy in a café
tied in knots by
representationality

While the byline
to the video
simply reads

*Offensive Surge
Clearing Lines*

just like that—

"clearing lines"

clearing lines—

That's as far as it got
that piece

Pax Americana

Taylor Swift and uh, the uh
Durability, um, of, uh, those
two words, *might* (might)

≈

And The Governors (The Governors)
uh, *Infra*, um, Rebel Province, um
Pax Americana, um, *yeah,* put *that*

≈

Poem's uh, wobbly (starting to), but uh, *ok*
um, ghost, uh, *ship*, Ghost Ship
um, goes uh, right uh, here (here)

≈

What do we have so far?
can we, um—fit, no it's *too*, uh
do microchips have colorful names?

≈

Ok ok, diplomat, *The* Diplomat, um
Taylor, uh, Demographic, um
scoot, no, ok—scoot, um, *infra* (here?)

≈

Rebel Province, that was uh, that uh
Pax—"a" "x" *common*, um
Ghost / Ship / Tour (tour?)

≈

Ok zoom out zoom out
what's with uh, the uh, *infra*
can we um, *feel,* still, the uh

≈

Demographics—*plural* (plural), like uh
The Lefts, The Rights, plural, um
Diplomat Majorette, *ok,* yeah

≈

Zoom in zoom in (zoom in)
Xi? *Xi* (with an "x") (x!)
how'd that all, um, *ok,* alright

≈

Durability, uh, let's uh, *lets uh*
squeeze, *infra,* like, um, *in,* like, uh
Chips? chips are uh, *not* touring, but um

≈

Taylor, just Taylor, like *that*
um, Structure, uh, super—no, um, *infra*
ok, what do we got now?

≈

Oh, Governors, of course, Governors
always fucking Governors
(always fucking Governors)

≈

No no no *keep'em,* keep'em
you know, keep'em on the uh, Ghost, um
the Ship! away—*away* from Taylor!

≈

So, um, *yeah,* pan over the um, the *whole*
Xi? yeah of course, Xi—in bold
Taylor too, um, you know, *They* Decide

≈

They Decide, and um, *yeah*
Demographic something something
ship uh, *ship's* um, adrift? *drifts*

Hominae Romanum

The popular meme is that
men think of the Roman Empire
at least once a day.

Senatus Populusque Romanum
stupendous aqueducts galore
badass sewers to spare.

"Yeah man, better to um
swear allegiance *now*
than drag this on."

Some love the helmet designs
others the Via Germanicus
cobblestones back to Rome.

Maybe some want slaves
secretly (women specifically)
their version of multiculturalism.

Maybe some just crave Bigness
in some generic way
instead of village squabbles.

Ask'em—what's on their minds
specifically, and do they—
do they dream of flowing robes?

Perhaps some covet
an unyielding marbled language

few can wield.

Surely a whole bunch suspect
a collapse of The Center
imminently upon them.

Whatever Rome means to men
specifically—to just one—
is vital intel, indeed.

Late Empire Casuistry

Then a hand on a windowpane
five stories above, seen from below
fingers—five, face coming into view
then eyes, no brighter than the hand
and that concludes this tale.

Oh, but not for some
some want the seeing of a hand
itself to anchor another tale
a deluxe tale involving (surprise)
the universe, that stage hog.

Others, want the hand itself
to be a sort of discerning eye
looking down below, surveying
assessing the present scene
sly enough to be *semi-detected*.

And then some want the face
and this is an old technique
to say hundreds of things
interpreted a thousand ways
towards a central Big Wow.

It appears too, some dispute
the five is actually "a five"
when one finger after the next
opens and plops itself on the pane
something they find spooky-sexy.

Then later, some are thunderstruck
by two eyes spying two eyes
down below, while looking up
dispassionate about building design
and the processes of glass making.

Poets of Shenzhen

Good morning poets of Shenzhen!
whoever you are (we've no clue).

In Cantonese or Mandarin
we'd send you a giant bonjour

from New Orleans—such as we are
flighty at times, but with stout hearts.

We ponder the start of your day
the things you do, would like to do

how it all sorts out (or doesn't)
what the glow of your deeds feels like.

Here, we're bodily in pause mode,
sluggish Louisiana mud.

The wage floor's—$7.25
folks grind all day, yet barely thrive.

We're even told Russia's to blame
if you can believe that (we don't).

Poets of Shenzhen! What's shakin?
are you hosting readings tonight?

at a school? at a library?
We're fond of bars, gardens, sidewalks

We're a boisterous bunch, but we're true!
we work with the mess given us.

We're often mired in foreign wars
we're coming apart by the hour.

Anyway, what's up with Hong Kong?
the scene there, just minutes away.

Baton Rouge, our state capital
can't be accessed by high-speed rail

Talk of rails—is 30 years old!
Homeless tents populate our streets

Still, though, poets from Baton Rouge
happily find their way to us.

Which of your poets reads tonight?
What's the latest styles? What's the vibe?

We flaunt (let's see) maybe 90
yeah, 90 styles, 60 poets.

Poets of Shenzhen! City sleuths
we're keen to know your best secrets

We're keen to be asked to read there!
Plane fare, a bed, some translators

I'm a veggie, requiring beer
My colleague, Henry—is veg too

Sean—like a *yue ren*, eats it all

We might not be the best of fits

Still, we're a striving bunch, fired up
we work with the mess given us.

Poets of Shenzhen! Esteemed peers
You're most welcome in New Orleans

Though we've no Bureau of Culture
no way to arrange a banquet

Still, these broken links, these *intents*
are the stuff of our poetics.

HUMANITAS

Humanity (a meandering raft)

Something here, won't allow
a simple phrase about Humanity.

Since Humanity is a dream
dreaming us, it floats, fragments.

So maybe this is a fragment
adrift in perilous waters

let's say, a swamp
at midday, in summer.

Here, our best portraitists
hold fast, hatch Humanity.

Here, our civilizational urges
find an outlet back to sea.

But, for now, this raft
is hushed among mangroves.

Something here, won't allow
a simple humanistic line

a seed of a workable society
a terrain of energies to integrate.

What is it that's disallowing
what is it that's speaking here?

Might the metaphor of waterways
signal the brink of beginnings

or might the dream of brinking
signal an open sea of endings?

Humanity (a quirky nomad)

"And not just across savannas
But into the canyons, and then
Out of the canyons, towards deserts
And beyond deserts, this cliffside.

People say this here cave's empty
But best scour the backmost nooks
That's where Fear is likely crouching
Warlocks of The End Times scheming.

The Warlocks stumble from the start
Lame attempts at conjuring awe
Frightening no one in this cavern
Panic builds up in their voices.

They scatter like a hundred bats
Out into the crisp morning air
Thank *mountaintops*, for crisp mornings
Lush meadows, meandering herds.

So we've settled in for a year
And sacrifice the passing days
Kindling verses, sparking up life
Popping off tales around the fire.

'Work the quirk!' everyone bellows
'Work the quirk!' *that* everyone does
But now, it's time to journey on
Taking with us cinders of heart

To the next valley where joy blooms
Or beachside where gloom goes to die
Where words crackle into the air
As the age funks out in ashes"

Humanity (a loose brick)

Dislodged a brick
from the cathedral
of Salamanca Humanism

—*that* was dodgy—

Took that brick home
put it on the mantle
stuffed it in the closet

—*that* was freaky—

Then took the brick back
reinstated that brick
when no one was looking

—*that* was sneaky—

And posted a photo reel
in the cathedral
with everybody looking

—*that* was cheeky—

Then lined up the words
*justitia, clementia
dignitas, abundantia*

—*that* was geeky—

And extrapolated
the governing concept
c o n v i v e n c i a

—*that* was ballsy—

Then transmogrified
the cathedral itself
into a black cat

—*that* was crafty—

The cat then pranced
all over town
nipping at hopes

—*that* was frisky—

Humanity (a glint in the fog)

Girls in white baggy pants
of linen, fluttering
crowd the boardwalk
no blouses embossed:
"stay foggy forever"

Boys in black tank tops
of rayon, rippling
crowd the boardwalk
no baseball caps embossed
"stay foggy forever"

The giant gilded golem
in leopard skin loincloth
at the edge of the bay
guarding the ancient city
gleamed in the fog, it seemed
for forever

Humanity (a squiggle)

In pencil, or pen, or blinking cursor:

These pyramid slabs
plopped down
slabbing it up

This cathedral's
cathedralizing
pre-cathedralization

This skyscraper's
got a long way
to scratch sky

We can see how the beautiful people
want the beautiful people
rendered in rock
with emeralds for eyes
diamonds for groins

People not procreating
en masse, on cue
sets the stage
for *specific* types
of rockwork

Yeah, from the squiggledom comes
all this and more:

Feathered headdresses in glass cases

70

Breastplate armor in glass cases
Suits and ties in a glass case
riddled in bullet holes

We can see how the gorgeous poems
from the gorgeous poem factories
roll out hot ready to be molded
into walls of Empire
about to crumble

The gorgeous poems hate the ungorgeous poems
though both are frantically conceived
in corners of chipped-up cities
of squiggledom
in a glass case

Humanity (a cretaceous terrace)

Municipalize electricity.

O for an island!

Plates lifting
plates sinking
plates crashing.

Federalize health industry.

O for an island!

Magma spewing
magma flowing
magma cooling.

De-monetize education.

O for an island!

Sponges chillin it
sponges chillin it
sponges chillin it.

Nationalize right to shelter.

O for an island!

Seashell clumps
seashell shards

seashell mounds.

Socialize childcare.

O for an island!

Sand crab pop
sand crab hop
sand crab bop.

Illegalize Billionaires.

O for an island!

Plesiosaur jaw
plesiosaur gut
plesiosaur turd.

De-privatize water & sewage.

O for an island!

Pterodactyls soaring
pterodactyls circling
pterodactyls diving.

Humanity (a celestial cluster)

Proximi Centauri
closest star to our sun
shines on nothing
at hand
not even an iris
yours or mine.

Proximi Centauri
has little to offer
but a name
two words
barely.

Look!
(not up there, here)
The cult of Proxima Centauri
has hatched—
one member, one 'like'
one comment:

"Rigil Kentaurus
so-called 'good folks'
—*fakers!*"

Humanity (a kind of churn)

But it was always that churn
of futile daily industry
that propelled them
alongside
the rocks, the logs, the sand
the guiding of water
the placement of trees
and a few other thousand
sub sub sub
enterprises

And needing abodes
(the sizes varied
the looks varied
materials into place
planned meticulously)
they did the abode thing
one might say

And that the aliments
consumed there
had to keep appearing
and not just appearing
but shared
along the way

Then the *enterprise*
of enterprises
the up up up
and away

into the future
the rearing
of this particular
(the name escapes them
though one
just smiled
at another
and seemed
a bit
perplexed
but confident
enough
to smile
again)

Congregated
then dispersed
over slabs of concrete
carefully arranged
a doorframe
we might say
to traverse

unto a sea of asphalt
unfolding
before their sight
and they think they must go
and go soon
together or alone

towards ocean's edge
called by a thousand names
none ever
quite

fitting
enough
for this...
for these...

sapiens
pop-outs with names
names that seem to hold
for the most part
like stonework
covered in vines and mold
or newly baking in the sun

at water's edge
churning
against the churn

Humanity (a sort of shape)

Because shaped-like-thats
can give hugs
to shaped-like-thats

And because
shaped-like-thats can hug
not-shaped-like-thats

And also because
shaped-like-thats are *also*
not-shaped-like-thats

And because also
not-shaped-like-thats
are *also* shaped-like-thats

It's a Huggy House
of shapes upon shapes
sorta shaping up

They had a sort of shape about them!
That people can say
They were shapely

ARTIFICIA NATIONALIS

Livewires & Duds

Seville woke up in New Orleans
and quickly spotted three poets
on its doorstep, sounding Northeast.

Benin rang the doorbell two times,
in came Havana flashing flesh
and three duds from Massachusetts.

A livewire from Port-au-Prince yelled
from across the rain-soaked alley
"two more duds closing in, east, west."

Seville said, "look, I'm a *livewire*
I can't just *ping* Ponchatoula
and make you all Bourbon Starlets!

And neither can Port-au-Prince *shine*
while two Connecticut duds croon
whatever they croon *shocking* themselves."

Benin, backing it up, added
"soon as these clouds clear, I'm *bouncin'*
plus activating—*four* livewires."

Havana, sprawled out on the porch
thinking of ways to *radiate*
without freaking a dud, or three.

Seville, stood on the balcony
and watched the rain turn to vapor

looking for livewires through the haze.

Port-au-Prince, fell in with two duds
dub-stepping to the riverbank
and tried—*confabbing*—a quick match.

Ponchatoula, woke up at noon
unaware of the whole circus
but *hungry* for the whole circus.

Aliens

In the 1890's, even 1790's
nobody was transfixed
by Martians

in that young nation.

Martians were the rage
in the 1950's.

Venusians, hit the stage
in the 60's.

The visitants, now, "at hand"
prefer *this side*
of the border.

The visitants, apparently, evade
330.904806 million of
330.904809 million

phone cams.

In the 70's
folks were transfixed
by that Earth pic

from space.

During the 1980's, 90's, and 2,000's
people's sense of agency

shriveled up.

This prematurely aged polis
by sundown forgets
the plot line.

These face-lifted ideals
this tummy-tucked, true
global position

welcomes aliens.

Terrestrials

Minoans leaping over bulls
in loincloths.

Truckers in Circle K's
showering.

Dolphins and Octopi
in green foam.

Roadhouse raucous night
Hattiesburg.

Single sail ship
toting tankards of wine.

Hangar selling firecrackers
exit 22.

A giant whorl of red
for a sun.

20 by 30 Stars & Stripes
at daybreak.

Undulating blue lines
for a sky.

F-15 sorties
return to Keesler.

Underground frescoed baths
galloping flautists.

Mothers in cut-off jeans
pack a twelve.

Pointy breasted damsels
snake in each hand.

Back seat rifle rack
F-450 truck.

Bronze double axe
on green marble.

30 ft. Unknown Soldier
at city center.

Black Minotaur lurching
on two legs.

Espectacularistas

for Swifties

Snaking lines—
out here's
anticipation's guts.

We want *something*
and now
even more.

Crowds cheering—
we're the same people
you know.

We want diamonds
refracting us
all night.

Doors opening—
in here's *everything*
not out there.

We want pinks
we want blues
we want golds.

Doors closing—
we can do that
and other things.

We want platforms
hovering above
and beyond.

Lights pulsing—
we do that too
re-colorize minds.

We want focus
up there
down here.

Vapor spouting—
funnels
corny cool.

We want song
from all sides
brushing up.

Floor trembling—
we're different folks
jostling together.

We want surprises
at choice moments
poking us.

Roof rumbling—
quivering mess
closing ranks.

We want insides
turned outside

turned inside.

Doors opening—
we can do that
totally, right?

We want reshuffling
of all feelings
and fortitude.

Elegies for Ancients

Elegy for chariots:

"m'kay yeah—
that *was* a run
rest tight now"

Elegy for a thousand arrows
followed by a thousand more:

"alright—
that's uh
plenty—
really"

Elegy for a bronze shield:

"look, we straight up didn't order this"

Elegy for a stubby sword:

"for sure—
if something comes up
we'll uh..."

Elegy for a proto-god
vying to become
a full blown:

"um...you're dead, right?"

Elegy for an imposing temple:

"stay down, man
you're *dead*, ok?"

Elegy for scattered inscriptions:

"no no no, no resurrections
sorry, wrong party"

Happy Campus

I.

This is the dirt-eating poetics that's gotcha
The dirt-eating poetics you've been yearning for.
You did good, you did something you hadn't before
Contorted yourself into optimal stances.
You persisted with your dirt-seeking impulses.

II.

When the garden trail came to a sudden dead end
You celebrated by dreaming as a log might
Calling forth decomposition's cute sister, life.
A single crushed can of rosé strewn thereabouts
Is all you, too, at maximum inflection point.

III.

But here you are back at the plazas of commerce
Into the routines of knowledge dispensation.
Here too you contort yourself to what's most pressing
These happy or grim faces of late empire's throng.
You do a sort of bump dance; attention glides up.

IV.

At noon, the plazas clear themselves of their contents.
Overhead, a Boeing seven-thirty-seven
Roars for curious ears; streaks of places to be
Fade, till the next industrial jolt wakens you.
Time for a quickie jaunt among ferns' spongy soil.

V.

This is the dirt-lavishing poetics at hand
A flexed forearm gripping a bulky book at dusk
Gives way to dalliance with penciled sprites at dawn
A picnic in the style of twenty twenty-two
Keen to supply lines of microchips and maidens.

VI.

FUEL is what's on tap today, sparking up form's forms
Combustions, pipelines, canalizations of fire
How the plazas themselves are poetical feats.
You can deem yourself a fallen log at midnight
Or rally the concrete under your feet to flight.

Two Seaside Elocutionists

I.

"This foam
is not a whisperer
of secrets

It's a splatterama
of hearsay
a vault of randomness

Powered by the moon
the old beast
is an auto-erotic

Optimator
is one name
Churner—another

Impervious to song
neglectful
of the portraiture

The sea—
is pure forgetfulness
in a storm of spontaneity"

II.

"This kelp—
makes for markets

far from these shores

Think chewing gum
think slippery soups
personal lubricants

Kind of just tossed
on these sands
about to rot

But imagine groves
whole forests yonder
swaying to and fro

Kelp—
is an elegant dancer
satisfier of many needs

Smooth Operator
is one name—
Big Squirt—another"

Two Maestro Bards

I.

"I need a walking stick, a strong staff
an estuary, reeds, daybreak sunlight
five kilometers of spongy paths

I need four hours of birdsong
the sound of cold, crashing waves
a cessation of sexual imagery

I need the marijuana king deposed
I need queen alcohol deposed
I need my ankle joints to hold steady

I need a tome of Tang dynasty poetry
I need to not recharge my phone
I need *one single line* of clean poetry."

II.

"You don't need a staff, man
a well-pruned public garden will do
fifty meters, well attended, is plenty

Birds can't be contracted to sing
crashing waves are in your head
you need *ass*—it's the staff of life!

Take a little puff why don't you
this beer's worth two weeks of life
not just ankles but your *neurons* too

You know Tang poetry's war poetry
plug your phone and look it up
it's all dirty empire stuff, poetry."

Prophets & Motels

And like—outta the blue, was like:

"Prophecy is visual and auditory.
Two shriveling motel palms.
Two systems can go wrong."

And then was like:

"Motel balcony ironwork
is boulevard crackwork—
prophets—prophyletize"

Saying shit like that, and like:

"Wail, kneel, bow
all you want—
motel fee—3 dollars"

Then like—oh my god:

"The green pool—is *your* place
an oasis, a mountaintop
motel executive suite"

And like—outta *nowhere*:

"Prophecy, you see—
now you don't see—
now you see (the motel)"

Random, right? then—*oof:*

"The sheets *were* washed—
we're a good motel
not a bad motel"

And then like—*ew*:

"Prophets in rooms
100 to 150—
motel policy"

Like *that*, if you can believe it, then:

"Graveyard motel clerks
are the true prophets—
till the next shift"

Rodrigo Toscano is the author of eleven books of poetry. His latest books are *The Cut Point* (Counterpath, 2023), *The Charm & The Dread* (Fence, 2022). His poetry has appeared in Best American Poetry (2023, 2004), *Best American Experimental Poetry*, *Boston Review*, *Poetry Magazine*, *The Kenyon Review*, *The Harvard Advocate*, *Georgia Review*, *Yale Review*, *Fence*, among others. Toscano has received a New York State Fellowship in Poetry. His *Collapsible Poetics Theater* (Fence Books, 2008) was a National Poetry Series selection. He won the Edwin Markham 2019 prize for poetry. He was an Honorable Mention for the 2023 International Latino Literary Awards. Toscano serves on the board of the New Orleans Poetry Festival. He was a National Poetry Series Finalist.

Whitman. Cannonball. Puebla.
by Rodrigo Toscano

Cover design by Rodrigo Toscano
Cover typeface: Avenir
Interior design by Laura Joakimson
Interior typeface: Adobe Garamond Pro

Printed in the United States
by Books International, Dulles, Virginia
Acid Free Archival Quality Recycled Paper

Publication of this book was made possible in part by gifts from
Katherine & John Gravendyk in honor of Hillary Gravendyk,
Francesca Bell, Mary Mackey, and New Place Fund

Omnidawn Publishing Oakland, California
Staff and Volunteers, Fall 2025
Rusty Morrison & Laura Joakimson, co-publishers
Elizabeth Aeschliman, production editor
Sophia Carr, production editor
Rob Hendricks, poetry & fiction editor
Jeffrey Kingman, copy editor
Sharon Zetter, poetry editor & book designer
Anthony Cody, poetry editor
Liza Flum, poetry editor
Jennifer Metsker, marketing assistant
Avantika Chitturi, marketing assistant
Angela Liu, marketing assistant

www.ingramcontent.com/pod-product-compliance
Lightning Source LLC
Chambersburg PA
CBHW011201090426
42742CB00020B/3415